YOU THINK YOU KNOW
GIRAFFES

Jane Hileman

Somewhere in Africa, there are giraffes...

Giraffes have **horns.**

 Giraffes have **ears**.

Giraffes have **eyes**.

 Giraffes have **noses**.

Giraffes have **mouths.**

 Giraffes have **teeth**.

Giraffes have **tongues**.

 Giraffes have **necks**.

Giraffes have **hair**.

Giraffes have **legs**.

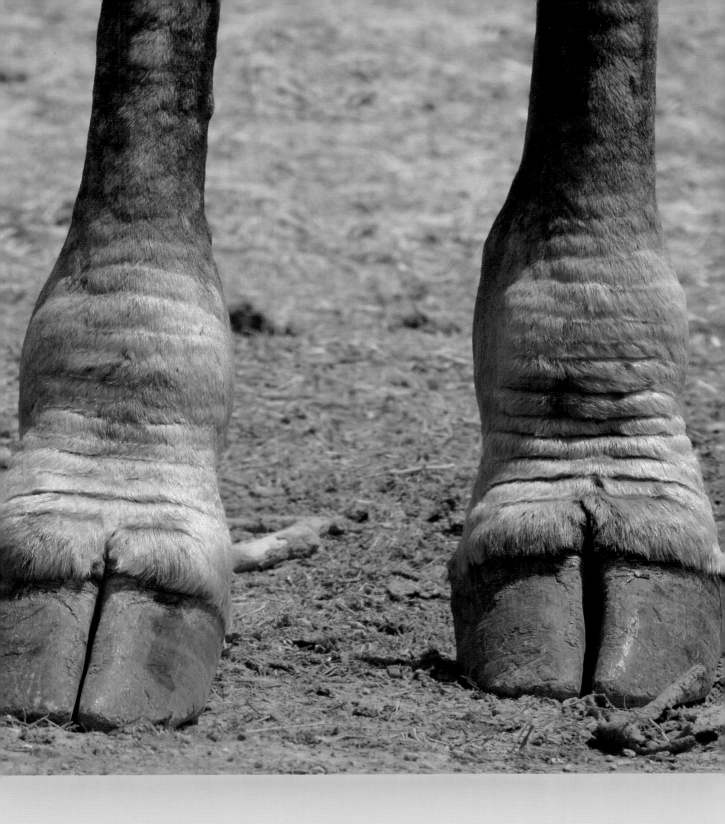

Giraffes have **hooves**.

Giraffes have **tails**.

Where Giraffes Live

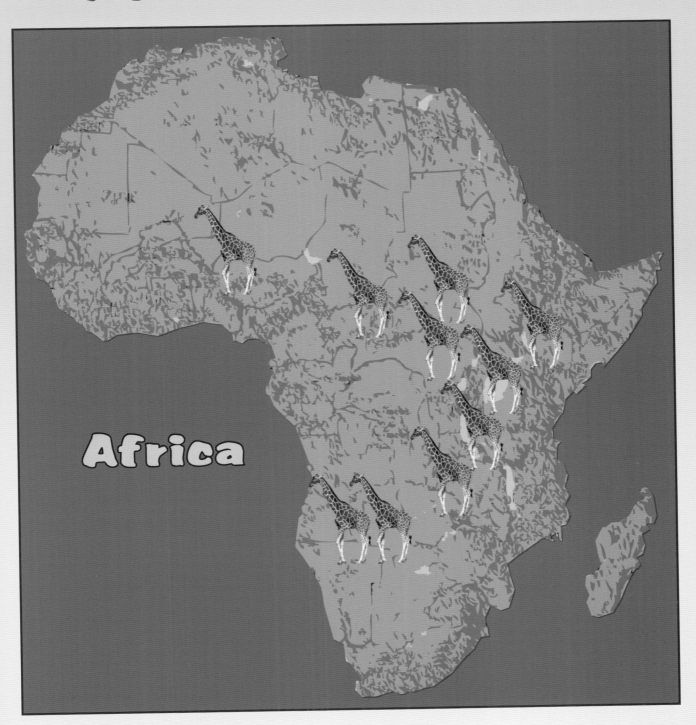

Africa

Giraffe Anatomy

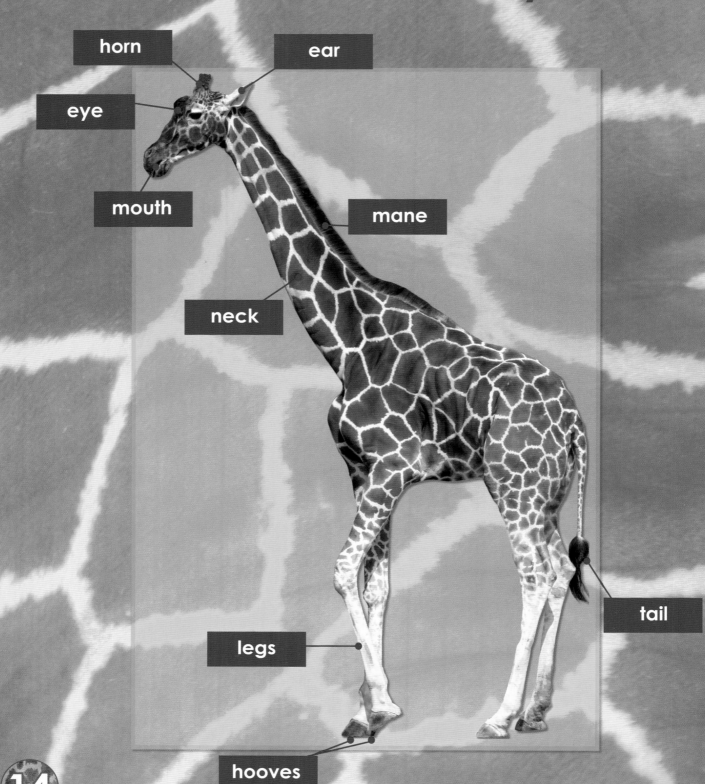

horn

ear

eye

mouth

mane

neck

tail

legs

hooves